AF443032

My First Photograph

This Is Me...

I was born on

At   o'clock

In

My name is

My name means

I'm called this because

My hair is

My eyes are

I am   feet and   inches tall

These Are My Parents

My mom is called

She was ______ years old when I was born

My dad is called

He was ______ years old when I was born

My mom and dad have known each other for ______ years

What mom says about dad

What dad says about mom

Mom says that I inherited her

While dad says I inherited his

Mom and Dad Today

Mom and Dad on the Day of Their Baptism

The Beginning of My Story

Mom's thoughts when she found out she was pregnant

How she told dad

His first thoughts and the first thing he did when he found out he was going to be a dad

How mom and dad told my grandparents and other members of the family

How they reacted

The names they thought about giving me

My Arrival!

The first thing mom remembers about the day I was born

____

____

____

____

____

The first thing she said

____

____

____

____

____

What dad remembers

How he felt

The first thing he said to mom

My Photographs

My Photographs

Why Baptism Is a Gift from My Parents

Why my parents chose to baptize me

How they prepared for my Baptism

My parents' hopes for me

How they plan to help me grow up to be a good Christian

Prayer

We thank You, O Lord,

for the children you have entrusted to us.

Help them grow in the faith they have been Baptized into.

Guide them in their important decisions in life

with the light of your Spirit,

so that they can bear witness to your love.

Amen

My Parents' Favorite Prayer Is

My Baptism

The day of the Baptism

When I was baptized, I was ______ months old

The ceremony was held in the ______ Church

The priest who baptized me was called

The psalms, prayers and letters from the Bible that he chose for me

What the Meaning of Baptism Is for My Family

Prayer

Blessed are you, O Lord, creator and Father,

for the day I saw the light of life

and through the waters

of Baptism was reborn as your son/daughter.

With your love show me the way

forward and guide me along the right path.

At every time and in every place may

I enjoy your friendship and bring joy

and hope to all, both near and far.

Amen

Prayer

O Lord, our loving Father,

who calls each of us by name,

help me grow in faith,

hope and love, by the example and intercession

of .... my Patron Saint.

Help me to fulfil my baptismal promises

and to recognize in every moment of my life

the signs of your Spirit, which you

give to me in our Lord Jesus Christ.

Amen

Being Baptized Means that I Promise to

My Photographs

My Photographs

My Godfather

My Godfather is called

He was born in   on

He was baptized on   at

Why mom and dad chose her

My Godfather's hopes for me and how she plans to help me grow up to be a good Christian

My Godfather on the Day of His Baptism

Me and My Godfather on the Day of My Baptism

My Godmother

My Godmother is called

She was born in   on

She was baptized on   at

Why mom and dad chose her

My Godmother's hopes for me and how she plans to help me grow up to be a good Christian

My Godmother on the Day of Her Baptism

Me and My Godmother on the Day of My Baptism

The People Who Came to My Baptism

The Gifts They Gave Me

My Photographs

Who Got the Most Emotional?

What Did my Baptism Mean for My Mom and Dad

My Photographs

After my Baptism, This Is How We Celebrated

The People Who Celebrated with Us

How I Behaved
During the Celebration

My Photographs

My Photographs

Illustrations

Elena Veronesi

Graphic design

Paola Piacco

WHITE STAR PUBLISHERS

WS White Star Publishers® is a registered trademark
property of White Star s.r.l.

© 2018 White Star s.r.l.
Piazzale Luigi Cadorna, 6
20123 Milan, Italy
www.whitestar.it

Translation and Editing: TperTradurre s.r.l.

ISBN 978-88-544-1244-6
1 2 3 4 5 6   22 21 20 19 18

Printed in China